First World War
and Army of Occupation
War Diary
France, Belgium and Germany

58 DIVISION
175 Infantry Brigade
London Regiment
2/11 Battalion
1 September 1915 - 21 February 1916

WO95/3009/6-7

The Naval & Military Press Ltd
www.nmarchive.com
Published in association with The National Archives

Published by

The Naval & Military Press Ltd

Unit 10 Ridgewood Industrial Park,

Uckfield, East Sussex,

TN22 5QE England

Tel: +44 (0) 1825 749494

www.naval-military-press.com

www.nmarchive.com

This diary has been reprinted in facsimile from the original. Any imperfections are inevitably reproduced and the quality may fall short of modern type and cartographic standards.

© Crown Copyright
Images reproduced by permission of The National Archives, London, England, 2015.

Contents

Document type	Place/Title	Date From	Date To
Heading	WO95/3009/6/7		
Heading	58th Division 175th Infy Bde 2-11th Bn London Regt Disbanded Jan 18 1915 Sep-1916 Feb and 1917 Jan-1918 Jan		
Heading	WO95/3009/6		
War Diary	Woodbridge & Melton.	01/09/1915	30/09/1915
Miscellaneous	2/XIth Battn. London Regiment.		
War Diary	Melton & Woodbridge	01/10/1915	28/12/1915
War Diary	Woodbridge	28/01/1916	28/01/1916
War Diary	Woodbridge	02/02/1916	21/02/1916
War Diary	Melton	21/02/1916	21/02/1916

wo 95
3009/6/7

58TH DIVISION
175TH INFY BDE

2-11TH BN LONDON REGT
~~JAN 1917 - JAN 1918~~

DISBANDED JAN 18

1915 SEP — 1916 FEB
AND
1917 JAN — 1918 JAN

WO 95
3009/6

WAR DIARY
INTELLIGENCE SUMMARY

Army Form C. 2118.

2/11 Battalion London Regt.

11/5/15

Hour, Date, Place		Summary of Events and Information	Remarks and references to Appendices
1		Bayonet fighting course construction.	W Grant & Co
2		Brigade Route March.	W.H.F.
3		Battalion attack on trenches.	W.H.F.
4		Bayonet fighting course construction.	W.H.F.
5		Church Parade.	W.H.F.
6		Entrenching. Final Assault Practice.	W.H.F.
7		Draft of 9 Officers proceeded to Mediterranean. Final Assault Practice.	W.H.F.
8	2 am	Zeppelin reported; CHELMSFORD & BRENTWOOD going N. "C" Co. turned out as B port Hand Grenade course. Course of Snipers. Two Companies moved to Antwerks at MELTON.	W.H.F.
	8 pm	Zeppelin reported. Battalion turned out to posts. Companies ordered to return, mostly arrived back at 4 a.m.	W.H.F.
9	2 am	Zeppelin reported. Battalion took up posts. Ordered back at 2.30 am on 10th. Cos mostly back at 4.30 am.	W.H.F.
	8.45 p.m.		W.H.F.

Westridge & Melton
September

6.30 am. — 4.30 p.m.

Army Form C. 2118.

WAR DIARY
1/11 Battn or Lowestoft
INTELLIGENCE SUMMARY.

1/11th BATT. COUNTY OF LONDON REGIMENT

(Erase heading not required.)

Instructions regarding War Diaries and Intelligence Summaries are contained in F. S. Regs., Part II. and the Staff Manual respectively. Title pages will be prepared in manuscript.

Place	Date	Hour	Summary of Events and Information	Remarks and references to Appendices
	10		Final Arsenal Practice.	WH Lawrence
	11		Training operations at MELTON.	WF
		3.30 p.m.	Zeppelins. 3 reported coming S.E. from KINGS LYNN. 3 reported to have left BELGIUM returning W. at 10.15 p.m. Batt. turned out 15 posts. Withdrawn at 2.30 a.m. (12th).	WF
	12		Church Parade. Zeppelin passed over WOODBRIDGE in a N.E. direction at 12 midnight (12-13th). Batt. turned out & withdrawn at 2 a.m. (13th). WF at huge alley observed at MAIDENSGRAVE.	WF
	13		Battalion (with transport) practice entraining.	WF
		At 8 p.m.	Batt. turned out for Zeppelins. Orders in at 1.25 am (14th). Bombs dropped at HEMLEY HALL. 1/11 Batt. Intelligence post under close fire. One officer flying Revolver Over (uninjured) Zeppelin seen in vicinity of SECKFORD HALL & bombs dropped.	WF
	14		Training MELTON CAMP.	WF
	15		Ditto. Zeppelin reported at LOWESTOFT. Batt. turned out to posts at 8.15 p.m.	WF
		9.30 p.m.	Orders to return to Quarters at 1.30 am (16th).	WF

1577 Wt.W10791/1773 500,000 1/15 D. D. & L.   A.D.S.S./Forms/C. 2118.

Army Form C. 2118.

WAR DIARY
or
INTELLIGENCE SUMMARY

(Erase heading not required.)

11th Batt. COUNTY OF LONDON REGT.

Instructions regarding War Diaries and Intelligence Summaries are contained in F. S. Regs., Part II. and the Staff Manual respectively. Title pages will be prepared in manuscript.

Weybridge & Purbright. September.

Hour, Date, Place	Summary of Events and Information	Remarks and references to Appendices
16	Under O.C. Companys.	MKRawlinson Col
17	Entrenching. Battalion warned at 11.20 p.m. that Battalion might be turned out for Zeppelins. Warning cancelled at 12.40 a.m. 17th – 18th.	WH
18	Draft of 52 men sent to 3/11 Battalion. Period of vigilance commenced at 7 p.m.	WH
19	Church Parade	WH
20	First Assault Practice. Stay Night.	WH
21	ditto	WH
22	Brigade operations. 3 Bat.s of Brigade against 7/11	WH
23	Route March.	WH
24	4g Batt entries new quarters.	WH
25	Kit & transport inspection.	WH
26	Church Parade	WH
27	Musketry.	WH
28	" Surveyed new defensive position near S.O.C.	WH
29	Division & O.C. Brigade. "Night" attack vicinity of KESGRAVE.	WH
30	Musketry.	WH

MK Rawlinson Col
Commr 21/X/15 London Regt

2/XIth Battn. London Regiment.

STATEMENT SUPPLEMENTARY TO WAR DIARY.

(a) TRAINING. Proceeding well. The Battn. has practised at one time or another every item of field training.

(b) DISCIPLINE. Much improved. Good in quarters and excellent at Drill and in the Field.

(c) (I) MEDICAL SERVICES. - Very efficient M.O.
(II) Veterinary Service. - Adequate.
(III) Supply Service. - Regular.
(IV) Transport Service. - In working order, but not complete in complement.
(V) Ordnance Service. - Our needs are now only Machine Guns and some equipment, e.g., entrenching tools.
(VI) Billets. - Good.
(VII) Channels of Routine. - Brigade Office routine well understood.

(d) ORGANIZATION. Four Company Organization in full working order.

(e) PREPARATION FOR IMPERIAL SERVICE. As Home Service men have left, all men in the Unit naturally are for Imperial Service. The Battalion, Minus 800 men found for 1st Btn., and Home Service men sent to Provisional Battn., is now much depleted and we look to the 3rd Line for repair of this wastage.

Lt.Col.,
Commdg., 2/XIth Battn. Ldn. Regt.

Woodbridge,
1st Sept. 1915.

WAR DIARY
INTELLIGENCE SUMMARY

Army Form C. 2118

of 1/1 Batt. London Regt.

(Erase heading not required.)

Instructions regarding War Diaries and Intelligence Summaries are contained in F.S. Regs., Part II. and the Staff Manual respectively. Title Pages will be prepared in manuscript.

Stamp: 2ND LONDON DIVISION — 5 NOV 1915 — GENERAL STAFF

Stamp: 11TH (RESERVE) LONDON REGT. 78

Place	Date	Hour	Summary of Events and Information	Remarks and references to Appendices
WOODBRIDGE & MELTON	OCTOBER 1		Forenoon Rifle and Convoy; Final Aircraft Practice; musketry.	Lt. Col. H. G. S. [signature]
	2		" " " "	
	3		Test inspection	
	4		Church Parade; Inspection of Rifles by C.O.	
	5		Company training; Attack & Anti-Artillery formations; Final Aircraft Practice; musketry; Flag of 4 Officers left for Westminster; Pratt turned out on air raid alarm returned to quarters 1.30 am 5th inst at 8.50 pm.	
	6		Capture of trenches by Bombing Pts.; Relieving Trenches, &c.; musketry; Final Aircraft Practice; musketry.	
	7		Specialist classes; musketry.	
	8		Brigade Route march; "	
	9		musketry.	
	10		"	
	11		Specialist classes; "	
	12		Church Parade;	
	13		Final Aircraft Practice; musketry	
	14		" " " " ; Specialist classes;	
	15		Battalion assault on Bigard Trenches; musketry; 3 Zepps. reported vicinity of Cromer. Batt. turned out & reassembled at 2.12 am fr 14 ins. Specialist classes.	
	16		Route march.	
	17		Company training; collected over work.	
	18		Church Parade;	
6.30 am	19		Specialist classes; Final Aircraft Practice; Hostile aircraft reported off SOUTHWOLD 10.25 am. Wireless corps laughing. J.B.C. & A. A.D.S.S./Forms/C.2118.	

WAR DIARY
2/11 (West London Regt)
INTELLIGENCE SUMMARY

(Erase heading not required.)

Army Form C. 2118

Instructions regarding War Diaries and Intelligence Summaries are contained in F.S. Regs., Part II. and the Staff Manual respectively. Title Pages will be prepared in manuscript.

Place: WOODBRIDGE & MELTON

Date	Hour	Summary of Events and Information	Remarks and references to Appendices
19		Final Grave Practice	W. Powell
20		Special Church	
21		Brigade Route March	
22		Manned new B.de. trenches, 2/11 in Reserve	
23		Kit inspection	
24		Church Parade	
25		Battalion entrenching TEMPE WOOD	
26		" " " " Third Armlet Practice	
27		Operations Orders; " " "	
		" " "	
		Aeroplanes entrenching : TEMPE WOOD.	
28		Aircraft attacked by searchers 8.35 p.m. Batt. ordered Alarm 10.5 p.m. Received 11.30 p.m.	
		horse Inspection.	
29		Brigade operation order 2/11 GRUNDISBURGH Alarm.	
30		Kit inspection.	
31		Church Parade.	

W. Powell Lt. Col.
Comg. 2/XI Batt. Lond. Regt.

OCTOBER

1875 Wt. W593/826 1,000,000 4/15 J.B.C. & A. A.D.S.S./Forms/C. 2118.

Army Form C. 2118.

2/XIst C. WAR DIARY of London Regt.
or
INTELLIGENCE SUMMARY

(Erase heading not required.)

Hour, Date, Place	Summary of Events and Information	Remarks and references to Appendices
Nov 16th	1 Officer proceeded overseas to join 1st line.	nil
" 18th	Inspection by OC Bn.	nil
" 22	Draft 29 Recruits sent to 3rd line.	nil
" 23	Field Inspection by OC Bn.	nil
" 24	Inspection of Transport & other Animals by ADVS.	nil
	Firing work new Anti-Aircraft pictures taken up.	
	Nothing else to report	

W H Fowler Lt Col
Comdg 2/XIst Co London Regt.

Army Form C. 2118.

WAR DIARY
INTELLIGENCE SUMMARY.
2/1 (Brigade Heading not required) London Regiment.

Place	Date	Hour	Summary of Events and Information	Remarks and references to Appendices
WOODBRIDGE	2 Dec 1915	11am	Grounds Officers met G.O.C. at GOBBLECOCK HALL.	
	13	9am	Battalion commenced digging defensive position in vicinity of GOBBLECOCK HALL & continued operations up to end of month.	
	15	11am	Order re "Unnecessary damage to property by troops" read to Batt.	
	17		Inspection of stores & mules by Maj. Richardson, D.T.O., War Office. Inspected by Remounts.	
MELTON	20		Lieut. J.R. Barry proceeded overseas.	
	28	11am	Inspection by G.O.C. on MARTLESHAM HEATH.	

Lawrence Major for O.C.
2/1st Batt. London Regt.

SECRET

Army Form C. 2118

WAR DIARY
or
~~INTELLIGENCE SUMMARY~~

2/XIth. (~~EAST~~ (d)..LONDON.."REGIMENT.

Instructions regarding War Diaries and Intelligence
Summaries are contained in F. S. Regs., Part II.
and the Staff Manual respectively. Title Pages
will be prepared in manuscript.

Place	Date	Hour	Summary of Events and Information	Remarks and references to Appendices
Woodbridge.	1916. Jan. 28.	10.0. p.m.	Zeppelins reported by Bde. H.Qs. No developments.	

Lt.Col.
Commanding 2/XIth. Battn. Lond. Regt.

Army Form C. 2118.

WAR DIARY
INTELLIGENCE SUMMARY

2/1×1 Bedfordshire Regiment.

(Erase heading not required.)

Instructions regarding War Diaries and Intelligence Summaries are contained in F. S. Regs., Part II. and the Staff Manual respectively. Title pages will be prepared in manuscript.

Hour, Date, Place		Summary of Events and Information	Remarks and references to Appendices
1916 **February**			
Woodbridge	2	20 Reservists reported.	
	21	54 " "	
Melton			
Woodbridge	22	Half Battalion moved to GRUNDISBURGH & BURGH. 203 Reservists reported. Transport moved to WOODBRIDGE.	
Melton			
Woodbridge	23	75 Reservists reported.	
	24	69 " " 4 Officers attached for training joined their own units.	

M H Beatty
Lt. Col.
Comg 2/1×1 Batt. Bedf.
Regt.

www.ingramcontent.com/pod-product-compliance
Lightning Source LLC
Chambersburg PA
CBHW081514160426
43193CB00014B/2688